USDA

United States
Department of
Agriculture

Forest Service

Pacific Southwest
Research Station

General Technical Report
PSW-GTR-239

January 2013

Life in Challenge Mills, Yuba County, California, 1875–1915, With Emphasis on Its People, Homes, and Businesses

Philip M. McDonald and Lona F. Lahore

Authors

Philip M. McDonald is a research forester (emeritus), Pacific Southwest Research Station, Western Forest Management Unit, 3644 Avtech Parkway, Redding, CA 96002; e-mail pmcdonald@fs.fed.us: and **Lona F. Lahore** was manager of the office at the Experimental Forest, Challenge, CA. Both are retired. They are members of the Yuba-Feather Historical Association, Forbestown, CA, P.O. Box 54, Brownsville, CA 95919.

Cover photographs: Original photos are on file at the Yuba-Feather Historical Association Museum.

Prologue

Special areas in many national forests have been set aside for research in the natural sciences. These areas are called experimental forests and are extremely valuable, especially for long-term research. In California, the Pacific Southwest Research Station has seven experimental forests that span elevational ranges from near sea level to about 9,000 feet on the west side of the Cascade, Sierra Nevada, and San Gabriel mountains, and over the crest to the 5,000- to 6,000-foot range on the east side. In places, they form a continuum with every major forest cover type included. This increases the worth of the experimental forests because the progression of vegetation and forest development over a large elevational range can be followed without interruption.

This report is about the people and their way of life in a small town in north-central California called Challenge Mills. It is surrounded by the Challenge Experimental Forest. This forest, dedicated in 1958 and now encompassing 3,500 acres, is situated in the foothills of the Sierra Nevada at the 2,500-foot elevation. The soil is best described as fertile, deep, and well drained. It is inherently forest land and ideal for the growing of trees, which are mostly ponderosa pine followed by sugar pine, Douglas-fir, California white fir, and incense-cedar. Native California hardwoods such as California black oak, tanoak, Pacific madrone, and Pacific dogwood also are present as individual trees or in groves. Research in forest ecology, silviculture, soils, and tree physiology at the experimental forest has resulted in more than 80 publications to date.

The saying "as goes the people, so goes the forest" applies well here. The people built a town, and used the land that became the experimental forest for wood products, food, water, and recreation. They traversed the forest with a railroad and other roads, harvested almost all the large trees, mined the streams, started forest fires, and were a major influence on the forest and its development. Understanding who they were, what they did, and when they did it provides valuable background for the research being conducted on the Challenge Experimental Forest today.

Abstract

McDonald, Philip M.; Lahore, Lona F. 2013. Life in Challenge Mills, Yuba County, California, 1875–1915, with emphasis on its people, homes, and businesses. Gen. Tech. Rep. PSW-GTR-239. Albany, CA: U.S. Department of Agriculture, Forest Service, Pacific Southwest Research Station. 55 p.

A shout of gold, the groan of oxen, the whoosh of lumber down a flume, the shriek of a locomotive whistle, the laughter of children, and the distress of unemployment—all portray the people and their activities in and around Challenge Mills, a small lumber-mill town in the foothills of the northern Sierra Nevada. This report is about the people of Challenge Mills and their way of life around the turn of the 20th century. Native Americans and Chinese are included among its residents. All are inextricably linked to one dynamic individual, Andrew Martin Leach, whose strong business acumen, along with his lumber mills, 50-mile flume, and 6-mile railroad, were the mainstay of the town. Over 20 homes and businesses are listed, and many colorful stories are told about what they were, where they were located, and by whom they were inhabited. This report also denotes the species of trees and the topography of the Challenge Experimental Forest and suggests its value to long-term natural science research.

Keywords: Challenge Mills, California, people, homes, businesses, Andrew Martin Leach, logging, lumbering, flume, railroad, experimental forest.

Summary

Historical documents are written in many ways. Some are lengthy and filled with facts and figures, while others are shorter, rigid, and to the point. This document is different. It focuses mostly on the way of life in the small lumber-producing town of Challenge Mills, California, located in the foothills of the Sierra Nevada around 1875 to 1915. It concentrates on the people: where they lived and how they lived with many small (perhaps not well-known) details about their social customs and especially their humor. Many colorful vignettes are told—some funny, a few sad, but always entertaining.

Times and dates are included where possible, and together with the adventures of the people, tell the history of the area. It begins with gold mining at higher elevations above Challenge Mills, describes transportation through Challenge, denotes specific activities of the logging and sawmilling industry, details the contribution of the patriarch of Challenge Mills—Andrew Martin Leach—and transcends to the boom and bust of his enterprise and eventually that of the town.

Chinese and Native American people are part of the history of the area, and they and their way of life contribute to the color and intensity of the town as well.

The foresight and energy of Andrew Martin Leach is a story in itself. Leach came from a Vermont family that was familiar with the dynamics of logging and lumbering. This background proved to be an advantage to Leach. When an opportunity to buy land and sawmills presented itself, he bought them; when the cost of transporting lumber and wood products to the only market available (in the Sacramento Valley) became prohibitive, he devised a long and expensive flume to get it there; when the cost of transporting logs to his mills became too expensive, he built a railroad; when his big mill at Challenge burned, he constructed two smaller ones.

Leach also had many valuable employees who contributed to his enterprise. Most were local residents, but a few came from far and wide. Most were poor by today's materialistic standards, but rich in terms of families, friends, and how they took care of each other. For example, when food was scarce, a deer was shared; when someone was ill, he or she was looked after; when someone died, he was dressed nicely and given a decent funeral.

A few of the not-so-common stories told by the oldtimers include snowshoes for horses, use of a gimlet (a small boring device) by teamsters for tapping whiskey kegs, obtaining title to land with an 18- by 24-inch cabin, the running of sawdust, turpentining, riding the flume boat, decorum at dances, buying groceries on the cuff, one night per week for bathing, and the politics of working on the roads.

In the 1890s, financial panic racked the business world, much like the "bubbles" of today. The harsh winter of 1889 and the panic of 1893 cost Andrew Martin Leach dearly. Burned sawmills, a washed-out flume, and borrowed money combined to ruin his enterprise—ending it in 1894. Today, Challenge has no businesses, and unless rebuilt, few habitable homes. Hopefully, the mapped townsite and related stories of the people mentioned here will help Challenge Mills to live on in memory of yesteryear.

Contents

Introduction

It started with the challenge: "I can cut more timber in a given day than you can," said a sawmill operator in northern Yuba County to a mill owner up the mountain. Although clouded in history as to who made this challenge, the name stuck; and the little hamlet at the foot of Pike County Peak became known as "Challenge Mills."

The history of Challenge Mills (reduced to Challenge in 1895) is more fascinating than fiction. Few locations can claim title to the "Old West" more emphatically than Challenge. Gold mining, lumbering, farming, fluming, railroading—all played a part in its history. However, a major part of the historical record at Challenge is that of its hardy and intrepid pioneers.[1] Their lives often were governed more by the basic need to provide for their families and keep a roof over their heads than anything else. At times, life was hard as the 1857 graves on a hillside overlooking what was then a pretty valley indicate (fig. 1). Undoubtedly, the work and play of families and individuals in this setting and in this era have been reported elsewhere. However, the authors have strived to describe the history of Challenge and the lives

The history of Challenge Mills (reduced to Challenge in 1895) is more fascinating than fiction. Few locations can claim title to the "Old West" more emphatically than Challenge. Gold mining, lumbering, farming, fluming, railroading—all played a part in its history.

Figure 1—Graves of Rachael (died January 4, 1858 at age 40) and Henry Hollomon (died December 23, 1857 at age 10 months) overlook what was then a peaceful meadow on the Challenge Experimental Forest. A four-line epitaph on each gravestone brought tears to the authors' eyes.

---

[1] Most of the material for this paper is derived from personal interviews by the authors of oldtimers listed under "Acknowledgments." Other sources, in descending order, were newspapers, diaries recorded by members of the Yuba-Feather Historical Association, and written histories.

of its pioneers, perhaps in more detail, and with more intensity, color, and humor than portrayed elsewhere.

Shortly after gold was first found at Coloma, California, in January 1848, the northern and central Sierra Nevada fairly exploded with prospectors. Gold was discovered at Bidwell Bar on the Feather River in 1849, and 20 miles north of Challenge on Rabbit Creek, now La Porte, in December 1850. By the summer of 1851, gold had been found in quantity at numerous locations in both the Yuba and Feather River drainages at the 3,500- to 5,500-foot elevation. Lesser amounts were found at lower elevations as well. In places, a piece of bare land became a tent town overnight, then a real town with permanent structures, and finally a supply point and place of refuge for miners when the winter snows closed their operations.

The "diggings," as the gold fields came to be called, could be rich, and the land along almost every likely stream was claimed and mined. At places the diggings were called "ounce diggings," meaning that with hard work, an ounce of gold could be attained by a miner in 1 day. Another early term to describe the richness of the site was "tincup," indicating that a tin cup full of gold was expected for a day's work. The gold was termed "free" in the sense that it was in the form of nuggets, flakes, and dust. Its extraction was called placer mining as opposed to hardrock mining where the gold was entombed in solid rock and needed to be crushed and accumulated before it could be used as a medium of exchange. Placer gold was collected in sluice boxes, pans, and cradles, and was the primary type of mining employed in the Challenge area. Two creeks near Challenge were mined: Little Oregon Creek to the southeast and Dry Creek to the southwest. The west branch of Dry Creek was particularly rich and was described as ounce diggings when first mined.

Some placers became huge depressions in the ground as the overburden and gold-bearing earth was blasted away with powerful streams of water. Challenge never had any large placers, but many towns at higher elevations did. Some placers had colorful names like Secret, Whiskey, Spanish, and Independence Diggings, and the towns near them were equally piquant, with names such as Port Wine, St. Louis, Scales, Howland Flat, and Gibsonville being typical. It was not until later that the gold in the streams was traced to its source in a mountain or under a lava cap. Here hardrock mines were located and lasted for a time.

Located at 2,500-feet elevation, Challenge was "on the trail" of all who journeyed above it in northern Yuba, southeastern Butte, and southern Plumas Counties (fig. 2). Not only was it a gateway to the diggings, it also was a place where several trails from the foothills came together. One route went from Marysville to La Porte via Browns Valley, Brownsville, Challenge Mills, Woodville, Clipper Mills,

> **Located at 2,500-feet elevation, Challenge was "on the trail" of all who journeyed above it in northern Yuba, southeastern Butte, and southern Plumas Counties. Not only was it a gateway to the diggings, it also was a place where several trails from the foothills came together.**

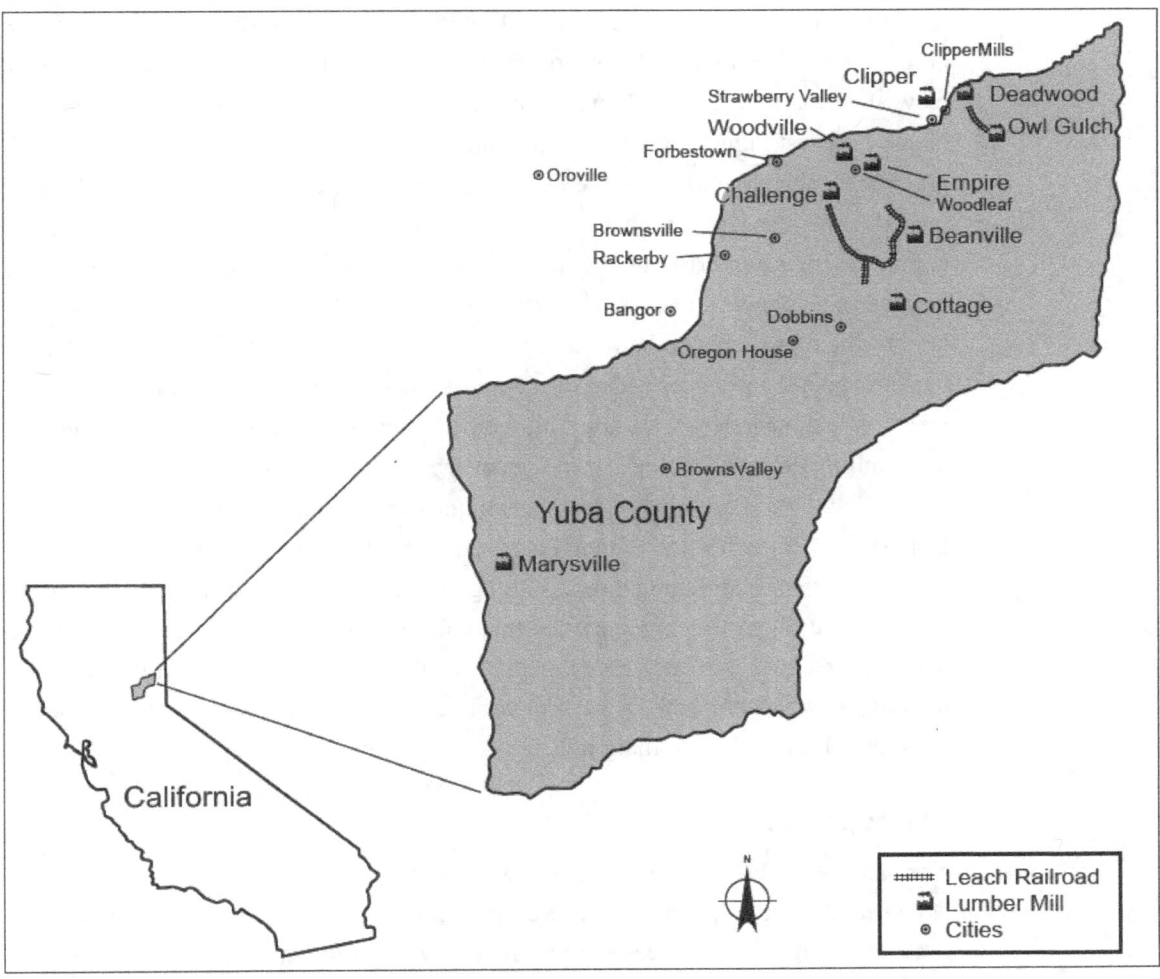

Figure 2—This sketch of Yuba County, California shows the location of Andrew Martin Leach's lumber mills and railroad.

Strawberry Valley, etc. Another route went from Oroville to Forbestown, Mount Hope House, Woodville, and on to La Porte with a cutoff to Challenge Mills. In terms of topography, Challenge lies astride a rather narrow ridge that separates the canyons of the North Fork of the Yuba River from the South Fork of the Feather River. Not only are the canyons deep, but also far below the ridgetops, and often involve a 1,500- to 2,000-foot change in elevation within a horizontal distance of 5 to 10 miles. Slopes typically are steep and covered with dense brush, oak groves, or forests. Rocky outcrops, precipitous cliffs, and steep slopes make travel across streams and ridges nearly impossible. Thus travel is along the main ridges, and this is as true of the Native American trails of centuries ago as it is of the paved high-ways of today.

For every entry about a mine or mill in the old ledgers, a record of forest fires is noted threefold. For example, one oldtimer noted on September 29, 1902: "The wind blew all night, which fanned forest fires in good shape. Challenge was in danger at one time last night. People got many things packed ready to go." It was standard practice for the citizens of Challenge to turn out to fight fire at least once each summer. Backfiring saved the town several times. It is not surprising that wildfire was common. Trees and brush hid the telltale mineral veins from the miner; vegetation impeded the logger in his quest to extract logs for lumber, and trees competed for land farmed for crops, orchards, and pasture. That fire was employed deliberately by some people to further their occupations is inescapable. Truth be known, people were just plain careless with fire. Many times, fires from the homes and ranches in the foothills below Challenge would get away, and whipped by the wind, burn all around the town. Early-day logging techniques and machinery also started fires from sparks or the friction of metal on rocks. Only the knot-free section of tree boles was utilized, and great masses of highly inflammable slash were left in the woods. Several old-timers mentioned that wildfires burned out of the southwest nearly every fall. The land survey of 1886 speaks to great length about the commonality of wildfires; some were ground fires, but others were devastating crown fires that blackened all in their path.

Transportation

The earliest routes into the mountains were primitive trails over which mules, horses, and pack trains journeyed. Rudimentary roads then were built, and with time were improved as streams were crossed with bridges and mudholes were filled with gravel. These often were toll roads, which tended to be better constructed and maintained than the earlier dirt roads, but they too were dusty and muddy, depending on the season. Toll roads typically were built by someone with money, like store owners or freight companies, who then charged a small toll to pay for the work. Much of the forest in northern California in the mid-19th century consisted of mile upon mile of virgin timber, broken only by rocky areas and the paths of old forest fires. Ponderosa pine and sugar pine were the most common trees in the Challenge area, with Douglas-fir, incense-cedar, and California white fir less common. Hardwoods like California black oak, tanoak, and Pacific madrone brought color and diversity to the landscape. The forest surrounding Challenge Mills was mostly virgin, often with large trees that contained a fortune in high-grade wood.

In the late 1860s, the demand for wood products was changing from declining use by the mines and towns in the mountains to increasing use by the burgeoning cities and industries in California's Central Valley. Transporting the product from the forest to the valley, a distance of 20 to 30 miles with a drop in elevation from 2,000 to 4,000 feet, was daunting. Lumber traditionally was transported by heavy wagons with six to eight horses in draft. Often two wagons with up to 12 horses were used. Each horse moved about 1,000 pounds of freight. Moving heavily loaded wagons downhill for many miles required a lot of braking, and in those days, wooden brake blocks were used. One enterprising fellow spent part of each winter making brake blocks for freight wagons out of sugar pine. One day he sold six pairs and they "went like hotcakes."

Transporting supplies and machinery to the many towns and mines in the mountains was a big job in the early days. Eight to ten wagons per day would pass through Challenge with some being double wagons joined by a short tongue. Fall was an especially busy time as supplies were sold to people who would be snowbound for the winter. One lady stated that her father was a teamster. "His teams were slightly different as he used both mules and horses. The lead animals were mules and wore bells so the wagons could be heard coming around the many turns of the road. A jerk line was used to guide the animals and a man had to be strong to use it. My brother and I would wait for the sound of the bells and run to see our father coming home. The animals made the trip so often that they knew their way home and did not need anyone to guide them the last few miles."

Where the roadway was steep, stage stops were stationed every 4 miles or less. These were not really stage stops but more accurately "freight wagon" stops where horses were changed. Just above Challenge the road was both steep and full of ruts. If the day was hot and the wagons fully loaded, the teamsters would drop the rear wagon in Challenge, pull the other wagon up the grade to the top, drop it there, unhitch the team, and return to town. If he had timed it well, he could overnight at the hotel, have a "snort" or two and a good meal, and swap "windys" with his fellow teamsters. While enroute, and he had a bit of dust in his throat, he remembered that small kegs of whiskey often were part of the backhaul up the mountain. Most teamsters had a gimlet, which was a little boring device. It was easy to bore into the top of the keg, use a small straw to extract the whiskey, and replace the whiskey with water. The hole was then plugged with axle grease that sealed and concealed the mischief.

Gold bullion from the mines was usually taken at night by a fast-moving team escorted by heavily armed guards on horseback.

In the early days, the town of Marysville in the Sacramento River valley was the main supply point for many towns and settlements in the extensive placer mining area around La Porte. One teamster hauled freight on this route for many years. He had one wagon and four big horses, and took 8 days to complete the journey.

Transporting supplies and machinery to the many towns and mines in the mountains was a big job in the early days. Eight to ten wagons per day would pass through Challenge with some being double wagons joined by a short tongue.

One time when he came home, he laid three $20 gold pieces on the table, much to the joy of his wife and children. That was a lot of money in those days.

The Marysville-La Porte road gained rapidly in elevation and often was beset with heavy snows in the winter. This led to a special feature of travel unique to the area—snowshoes for horses, introduced in 1865 (fig. 3). At first, square wooden plates were used, but the damp snow clung to the wood and made them heavy and awkward. Iron was then substituted, followed by thinner plates of steel with rubber lining on the bottom for which the snow had no affinity whatsoever. The plates were 9 inches square, and fitted to the horse's hooves. They had to be fitted to each horse, as their feet varied in size—a task that took about 2 hours for one man to shoe a four-horse team. When first put on, some of the horse's legs were cut above the feet, but they soon learned to adopt a wider stance to avoid this malady. A few became good snow-horses at once, most took a while longer, but others seemed incapable of learning to use the shoes at all. One correspondent mentioned that "Some of those horses were smarter than I was. My father had one that sat down. Yes, he sat down and held his foot up. A lot of people didn't believe this, but we have a picture of it."

> **A special feature of travel unique to the area was snowshoes for horses, introduced in 1865. At first, square wooden plates were used, but the damp snow clung to the wood and made them heavy and awkward. Iron was then substituted, followed by thinner plates of steel with rubber lining on the bottom for which the snow had no affinity whatsoever.**

Figure 3—In the heavy-snow country above Challenge, the horses actually wore snowshoes to get the mail through. The story goes that one horse actually sat down and held his feet up to facilitate the process.

In the winter, sleighs were used. If the snow was shallow, sleighs were pulled by horses with no snowshoes, and then as the snow became deeper, horses with snowshoes. Snowshoes or no snowshoes, there were times in the winter when no animals could get through. The teamster then would strap on his own snowshoes and pack the mail on his back to the next station. No one told him to do this; he simply did it because it was his job to do. "My father would grow a beard in the winter to keep his face from freezing" said one lady. The company that had the contract paid him $60 per month to deliver the mail.

Travelers, usually singles or couples, were the main occupants of the stages, along with varying amounts of freight. A four-horse stage ran from Oroville, through Challenge, to La Porte and carried six to eight passengers. Stage stops were located every 4 to 12 miles along the road, depending on the grade, either to change horses or to feed and water them. At major stops, pork, chicken, or beef and "fixins" was standard fare for travelers, with an occasional haunch of venison, steak of bear, or mess of trout thrown in. Homemade pie was a treat and doughnuts were worth their weight in gold. People who traveled in the dry season were subject to clouds of dust. To counter this malady, most everyone wore a duster, which was a light coat. Women travelers also wore a veil over their hats and faces. Winter travel often was precarious with washouts, deep snow, and fallen trees impeding the right-of-way. The *Marysville Appeal* of November 19, 1915, noted: "The Marysville-La Porte stage line has started on its winter schedule of leaving Marysville at 3 o'clock in the morning instead of at 4, which is the time of departure in the summer. On account of the bad roads of winter, it takes several hours longer each day to make the trip." Winter wasn't the only time that accidents could happen. On March 2, 1903, a run-away was noted: "Smashed up the stage, seriously hurt two horses, and slightly injured the driver."

Over the years, Oscar and Julius Pauly had several stage routes in northern California. They began work in the transportation business beginning about 1880, at first driving freight wagons and then stagecoaches. Sometime later, Oscar had the dubious distinction of being held up by Black Bart.[2] "He took everything from the stage and the passengers too." Oscar also was one of the first people to see Ishi.[3] On one of his runs in the summer of 1911, he noticed a wild-looking fellow huddled against a fence who didn't have any clothes on and looked like he was in trouble. He then called the sheriff, who fed and clothed him.

There were times in the winter when no animals could get through. The teamster then would strap on his own snowshoes and pack the mail on his back to the next station. No one told him to do this; he simply did it because it was his job to do.

[2] Black Bart, alias Charles E. Bolles, was a notorious stage robber who operated in the Marysville-La Porte area in the early 1880s. He always wore black clothes, a black bandana over his head, and a black hat, hence his name.

[3] Ishi was the last member of a "lost" Indian tribe (Yahi) who lived in the foothills of several counties in north-central California. He was befriended by anthropologist A. L. Kroeber and his wife, Theodora, who documented his way of life and that of his people.

There was no welfare in those days and employers tended to take care of their people. For example, the Paulys kept several employees on the payroll for years whether they worked or not. One long-time and valuable employee was a Native American, who had a very large family. Oscar supported the entire family for years.

Around 1910, the Paulys had at least 10 stages; 8 operating and 2 in reserve. From about 1900, the mail was delivered by virtue of star route mail contracts, which were bid for every 4 years. Each stage coach had "Wells Fargo Express" displayed on the sides because they always carried Wells Fargo material along with the mail. A big help monetarily were passengers. Oscar always got his passenger franchise from the State of California Public Utilities Commission, and in his words "owned" these routes. In 1914, he was the first one to drive an automobile on the star route mail lines. His first trucks were black Model T Fords, and then a Reo, followed by a Federal. It had a chain drive and hard rubber tires. It was no surprise that Wells Fargo bought every one of the stagecoaches when the Paulys switched to automobiles. Wells Fargo got a lot of good publicity out of those coaches. At first, gasoline was hard to come by and Oscar had a 150-gallon tank in back, but it wasn't a problem for long.

"Julius and Oscar gave an awful lot of free service to people along the route," remarked a son. Many times, local citizens would give them a shopping list and ask them to pick up items in town and deliver them to places along the way. Of course, they were paid for the items, but given nothing for shopping or delivery. There was no welfare in those days and employers tended to take care of their people. For example, the Paulys kept several employees on the payroll for years whether they worked or not. One long-time and valuable employee was a Native American, who had a very large family. Oscar supported the entire family for years.

For local transportation, people walked or rode on horseback. A 2-mile walk was regarded as nothing, and 5 or 10 miles on a horse was thought of as being equally easy. For longer trips, say to town, a two-horse wagon was used. A wagon was a necessity as a load of supplies often needed to be hauled back home. Only well-to-do people had buggies, and not many people in Challenge had them.

People and supplies were not the only users of the road. In 1910, about 3,000 head of cattle went through Challenge on their way to higher elevations. About 30,000 sheep made the journey that year as well. The sheep traveled all the way to Quincy in Plumas County where the lambs were sold. They then left Quincy, circled down through Downieville, and eventually to the foothills where the home ranch was. Some sheepmen began their trek at Downieville and ended at Challenge. Jim and Charley Brown ran big bands of sheep. As for cattle, a man named Carmichael ran 1,000 head, and another with the moniker Scott moved about 500 head into the Howland Flat area before 1910. Other ranchers ran cattle into the Lost Creek country as well. Like one gentlemen said: "In general, the cattlemen and sheepmen had no trouble, largely because this was big country and there was room for all."

Like most small towns at lower elevations in the Sierra Nevada during 1875 to 1915, a network of small roads radiated out from Challenge Mills. They linked small settlements and homes and farms of individuals to each other and to the town itself. Some of these inhabitants were Native Americans, Chinese, and a few rugged individuals.

Native Americans

The Native Americans associated with the Challenge area were the Maidu or more specifically Southern Maidu. Because no large encampments in the local area are known, their occupancy apparently was more transitory than permanent. Plentiful game and a plethora of acorns and berries in the fall guaranteed their presence during this season, and numerous holes in several large rocks attest to the grinding of acorns. Over the years, a few obsidian arrowheads have been found that indicated hunting for both deer and birds.

The Maidu had a high degree of social organization in terms of hunting, food gathering, worship, and especially basket weaving. Their baskets were the coiled type, made of peeled willow or unpeeled redbud (*Cercis* spp.). Nellie was a familiar Native American woman in the area. She made beautiful baskets that were finely woven with various designs and shapes. She even covered a bottle with a fine, tightly woven design with hinges for straps to be inserted. It took Nellie 4 years to weave a large basket (fig. 4) to burn in a special ceremony honoring her dead husband. A local woman saw the basket and said that no husband was worth burning a beautiful basket like that. Nellie replied "You bad women you."

The Maidu burial ground (a small one north of Challenge) was enclosed by a pole fence and within this enclosure were wooden platforms about 10 feet high with cross bars on each. These cross bars held the clothes and food to be burned for the departed. The cross bars contained shirts, shoes, pants, and hats for the Indian men; waists with no buttons, skirts, and bandanas for the women; and smaller items for the children. A neighbor said that she could hear the participants wailing and mourning all night.

The mourning anniversary known as "burning" or "cry," as practiced by the Southern Maidu, took place annually in early autumn, about September or October, often on the cemetery site or near it. The purpose of the ceremony was to supply the dead. The amount of property destroyed must have been immense by aboriginal standards. At one burning in northern California, Kroeber (1976) remarked "As late as 1901, 150 poles of baskets, American clothing, and the like were consumed at a single Maidu burning. Each family prepares its own poles, which are strung from top to bottom with objects of one kind or another. Larger articles and quantities of

It took Nellie 4 years to weave a large basket (fig. 4) to burn in a special ceremony honoring her dead husband. A local woman saw the basket and said that no husband was worth burning a beautiful basket like that. Nellie replied "You bad women you."

Figure 4—This exceptionally large and beautiful basket was woven by Native American Nellie Johnson to be filled with items that, after burning, would comfort her husband in the afterlife.

food are placed at the base of the pole. The ceremony lasts a night and a day. Beginning in the evening, the participants sit in a circle for an hour or two." One visiting White lady stated "not a whisper could be heard, the atmosphere was profound, and all my religion came back to me." Later, she shed a wealth of tears for a young girl who had died a few months earlier and was being remembered.

During the night, each group of mourners remembered its dead and sang its own songs, independently of the others. At the first sign of dawn, the poles were lifted down and the objects stripped from them, and thrown into the fire with much swaying and wailing. This plainly was the climax of grief.

Part of the ceremony was to place items in the basket that could be used in the afterlife. One gentleman mentioned that some items were gotten from the Challenge store. The proprietor looked forward to the Native Americans visiting the store, whereby a single boot, a small pair of pants, one work glove, some very old smoking tobacco, and other items of a similar nature were cheerfully extended at a very reasonable price. Obviously, the items were more symbolic than for everyday use. However, in her diary of October 30, 1896, one young lady joyously noted "Father bought two baskets for me. They had not burned yet." Consequently, at least a few "treasures" must have been placed in the baskets.

Chinese

A small Chinese settlement was located on the northeastern outskirts of Challenge in the 1880s and 1890s, and burned in 1905. It consisted of a small store, a building for gambling, and several cabins. A typical cabin consisted of one room and housed five or six Chinese. They usually had a garden enclosed with sapling poles to keep out the deer. They would carry 5-gallon buckets (kerosene cans) from the stream to water their gardens. At the garden, they would use smaller cans with holes punched in the bottom for sprinkling cans. They cooked over their fireplaces, which were built of rocks and local clay. At least one cabin had an exquisitely decorated jar that contained sticks of incense, which were lighted after dark each night to ward off evil spirits.

Most inhabitants were single men, but a notable exception was Jim Ah Wah, who had six children. Jim, who was well known in the community, died at age 60. His obituary was noted in the *Marysville Democrat* of March 2, 1897. Most of the Chinese worked at whatever they could find. They may have helped to build the railroad. Some eked out an existence scratching for gold, and evidence of their work has been found along the east fork of Dry Creek and in the gulches and draws of upper Little Oregon Creek. They were hard-working and very thorough miners who gleaned gold from cracks and crannies that the early miners had missed.

Another Chinese citizen of note was Lum—a solitary Chinese gold miner who lived on the west fork of Dry Creek. Lum had a small cabin there. He liked to play pool and borrowed a pool table from Ray Gordon, of the pioneer Gordon family who lived nearby. Lum also liked children and always had candy for them. Indeed, local children would find some excuse to go by his cabin as often as they could. He liked one lady and every spring he would bring her a Chinese lily in a dish filled with rocks. In return, he was directed to go out and catch a chicken for dinner.

One lady mentioned that the Chinese had a small cemetery across the road from their settlement. Apparently, they also believed in taking care of their ancestors and would place food in small dishes at the head of the graves. However, as soon as possible, the bones were interred and sent back to China. Not a trace remains today.

A couple of miles south of Challenge was a small community of Chinese men, who mined a small tributary of Dry Creek for 2 or 3 years. It only flowed in the winter, but apparently was next to an area of shallow bedrock that was rich in gold. One oldtimer remembered selling a 200-pound hog to the Chinese for one dollar. Another oldtimer recalled that the Chinese wanted what we would now call "liver galls," probably for use as a medicine. They would pay neighboring boys 50 cents for a rattlesnake gall and 25 cents for a skunk gall. That was a lot of money for a "young-un," so several would carry a big stick to and from school and a thread in

Lum liked one lady and every spring he would bring her a Chinese lily in a dish filled with rocks. In return, he was directed to go out and catch a chicken for dinner.

their hat band with which to wrap the gall. Consequently, the population of both these creatures decreased dramatically in the area for a time.

One local fellow spent many a day prospecting deep in the wilderness. One time while lost, he stumbled on a small cabin in a remote area inhabited by an elderly Chinese man, who seemed rather lonely. As it was late in the day, he was invited to dinner and to spend the night. After a pleasant evening and much talk about gold mining, he heard the unmistakable sound of a rattlesnake. The Chinese man also heard it and went over to a corner of the cabin, loosened a little knot in a board, and up popped the head of a very well-fed, full-grown rattler. "Not to worry, not to worry" said the Chinese "he my friend, I feed him." Understandably, the fellow did not spend that night or any other night in the cabin.

One rugged individual owned property north of Challenge, grew several crops, and raised sheep. A forest road bears his name today. He was described as a real character by a person who knew him as an older man. The story goes: "I remember the old fellow. He never took a bath. He would come to the store to buy a new shirt, but he left the old one on. The old one would rot away and he would reach in under his undershirt to pull out pieces. He used to wear stag overalls. They were the color of red dirt (the color of the native soil in the area). I remember his cabin; part of it fell over. He just moved an old water trough in under the edge of the cabin. That was where he slept. He would say if Christ slept in a manger, why he could sleep in a water trough." He just smiled when someone remarked that he hoped the drain in the trough was open when it rained.

African Americans

Not many African Americans lived in the Challenge area. However, one well-liked fellow lived just south of Challenge. He was a former slave, quite old, had a beard, and read the Bible all the time. He would come over and stay with one family's children when the parents went to the dances.

Spanish Explorers?

Stories of a very early (1600–1700s) Spanish presence in the area persist. For example, a logger fell into a small tunnel or mine shaft and found a piece of armor like that worn by Spanish soldiers. A miner found an old shovel and part of a firearm at the bottom of a deep natural shaft where the 19th century miners could not have been. The *Marysville Appeal* of October 14, 1915, stated "The first White men could have been Spanish as they passed through to a rumored gold mine north of Challenge." No record of Spanish explorers or soldiers being this far north in California during this period are mentioned in the history books, but the stories persist, are tantalizing, and might even be verified someday.

Challenge Mills—Early Days

Challenge as a hamlet did not exist until about 1862, when a small sawmill at Strawberry Valley, located about 10 miles up the road from Challenge, was moved to the relatively flat ground just west of the present-day school. Union Lumber Company was the owner. This company was truly a pioneer industry in the Challenge area. It was established in 1852 by W.K. Hudson and Samual Harryman as Hudson and Company. It then went through several ownerships and name changes until 1864, when it officially became the Union Lumber Company with W.K. Hudson, president, and A.P. Willey, vice president (Thompson and West 1879). By 1873, the Union Lumber Company had 15 mills in Yuba County and manufactured 4 to 6 million board feet of lumber annually.

The Union Lumber Company eventually sold this sawmill, several others, and all their timberland to Andrew Martin Leach. Here some confusion exists. We know that Leach began negotiations with Hudson and Willey of the Union Lumber Company for most of the land and mills in 1873 and 1874. We believe Leach acquired the Challenge mill in 1874. Purchase of the remaining land and mills was consummated by 1879.

This web of ownerships and the frequent relocation of mills were typical of the industry in the early years. At first, the product from the mill was sold "at the saw"—meaning that the demand was nearby. It also meant that logs for the sawmill were nearby as well. And because the early mills were powered by water, a stream or pond in close proximity also was mandatory. The mills themselves were relatively simple and usually contained a single circular saw that cut 4,000 to 20,000 board feet daily (Cronise 1868). As the timber was cut, the logs had to be moved from farther and farther away. Eventually, the available timber was gone or the distance of moving the logs was too great, and a new tract of land was needed. Sale to a new owner and the moving of the mill often occurred at this point. Moving the dismantled mill, usually by a "sled" or heavy wagon pulled by horses, was a fairly easy task.

Transporting the logs from the woods to the mill was by oxen, with four or five yoke to a team (fig. 5). They pulled heavy wagons, called trucks, which usually carried just one or two large logs. The four wheels on the trucks were made of solid wood and sheathed with iron rims. Of course, when dry, the wood shrank and needed to be tightened up with wooden pegs. Even then, they "made quite a chuckling noise when rolling along" said one oldtimer. Each ox wore a heavy yoke across his shoulders and a chain that fastened him to the next ox. They also had rather large and sharp horns that could be dangerous. Instead of sawing them off each year, one operator placed round brass tips on them that sparkled in the sunlight. The

Challenge as a hamlet did not exist until about 1862, when a small sawmill at Strawberry Valley, located about 10 miles up the road from Challenge, was moved to the relatively flat ground just west of the present-day school.

Figure 5—The size and number of logs, and method of conveyance by oxen and truck, were typical of the Challenge Mill era. Henry South (by wheel) worked for Andrew Martin Leach for years.

animals were powerfully built across the shoulders and capable of moving amazing loads. The oxen were driven mostly by talk and an ox-driving stick. Each ox knew his name and worked by it. No one beat the oxen with the stick, but prodded them if they didn't work on command. Like mules, oxen could be temperamental and sometimes required a little sweet talk. One oldtimer drove an ox team for Leach for many years and then for another mill. One cool morning, the oxen had to pull a loaded truck up a short, but steep, hill near the mill. They moved right along until they got to the base of the hill, and after that, not one step further, profanity and pleading notwithstanding. Another oldtimer was summoned. He went up one side of the team and down the other, put his arm around each ox, and softly called it by name. Then he went behind the team, let out a yell, and up the hill they went.

The standard method for loading the logs onto the truck was with a "crosshaul." This was facilitated by cutting a small trench into the hillside next to the truck and just slightly above it. Logs were piled just above the trench, and by means of peaveys and bars (fig. 6), individual logs were hand-rolled into the trench and onto the truck. Larger logs were loaded with the help of oxen. The first members of the team were unhitched, placed on the other side of the truck, and used to pull (crosshaul) the logs onto it.

Figure 6—Woods workers and their tools: from left: bucket of water and tin cup, cant hooks, log jacks, ax, and peavey (point on end of handle).

Andrew Martin Leach

The saga of Challenge Mills begins about the time that Andrew Martin Leach began to acquire land and mills. Indeed, there probably would never have been a Challenge Mills as a community had it not been for Leach. Of course, where there is industry, there are jobs, and income, and money to be spent. In turn, the industry and its employees need homes and supplies. Because Leach was the kingpin of the community, we begin by describing his operations; portray some aspects of life in Challenge at that time; transcend to the businesses, homes, and people of Challenge during the next 40 years; and end with the decline of Challenge as a town.

Born December 7, 1841, Andrew Martin was one of three children from a prominent family that had extensive lumbering interests in Vermont (Leach 1925). Andrew Martin (fig. 7) arrived in the foothills of Yuba County in 1863, and started to build his lumbering empire. As noted earlier, he began purchasing sawmills and timberland in 1873, and by way of negotiations that became final in 1879, became owner of the Deadwood, Cottage, Clipper, Diamond Springs, Empire, Woodville, and Challenge mills, and cutting rights to many acres of timberland. A few years later, he owned at least 3,500 acres outright (Mansfield 1918). Later, Leach constructed two additional mills: Beanville (built about 1888) and Owl Gulch (built about 1892). A colorful story is told about how Leach acquired some of his holdings. In those days, 160-acre homesteads could be claimed by building a cabin 18

Figure 7—Andrew Martin Leach. Photo taken at Woods Photographic Art Gallery, Odd Fellows Building, Marysville, California, 1878.

To obtain land Leach had several cabins built 18- by 24-inches in size, with a handle on top, that were placed in the middle of vacant government land by employees. After the claim became recognized as legal, it was then turned over to Leach.

by 24 feet in size and living in it for 5 years. Leach had several cabins built 18- by 24-inches in size, with a handle on top, that were placed in the middle of vacant government land by employees. After the claim became recognized as legal, it was then turned over to Leach. An oldtimer stated that "This is how my uncle home-steaded 120 acres for Leach." Another remarked the law at that time was such that a person could claim everything he built a fence around, so he built a fence "by falling one tree and then another end-to-end, and claimed both sides of it."

A more common way of acquiring land was to have Leach employees file on a quarter section, furnish them with lumber to build a real cabin, issue them some groceries from his store in the winter months, and attend to all legal requirements connected with homesteading. When they had lived on the land long enough to get a title, he would give them a small amount of money and have them sign their land over to him.

When Leach first bought the Challenge mill, it was rather small and cut about 18,000 board feet per day. With continuous enlargement and the installation of a steam engine and boiler, production increased to 40,000 board feet per day (fig. 8). Employment jumped from a few men to over 50. In the course of expansion, the mill became a complex of over 20 buildings and the support center for all of Leach's mills and machinery. It is not clear if 50 men included the workers that were employed in felling the trees and bucking them into logs, and skidding, loading, and transporting them to the mill during the "season." Six to eight months generally comprised the season, no work being done in the winter.

Figure 8—Leach sawmill and crew at Challenge, California, in 1885. Note barrels of water on roof to quench potential fires.

In addition to the sawmill, the Challenge mill complex contained numerous out-buildings including a company store, Leach's home, office, boiler house, blacksmith shop, and huge warehouse, at least 200 feet long. The company store was described as having all kinds of tools and groceries where his employees, contractors, or even residents could get their supplies. The blacksmith shop was described as being state-of–the-art for its day. One correspondent recalled that just west of what is now the Yuba-Feather Union Elementary School "immense quantities of lumber were by the side of a balloon-shaped railroad track, one-third of a mile in length." Barns and loafing areas for oxen and horses were nearby, with one oldtimer indicating an area across the Marysville-La Porte road where a deep well for watering stock had been dug. At least two correspondents mentioned a Leach bunkhouse for single men that was located just north of the mill complex.

Apparently anyone could buy what they needed at Leach's store, which was the only store in town. Often, credit was given in the form of script. Although the company owned the store, Challenge was not a company town in the sense that the company owned the houses. Clearly, people owned their own homes on their own property. The store carried just about everything imaginable, including groceries, work clothes, boots, and tools. Miners traveling to the mines above Challenge were good customers. They lived mostly on sardines and mackerel, which required no more work and time away from mining than to open the can. Boots and material for tents also were good sellers. Many miners made their own tents out of yard goods and sail needles. One lady noted "The store also carried fabrics, and for those who could afford it, each child would choose material for a dress. However, most of the time, mother made our clothes from dresses given to her by friends. The dresses were made over and handed down many times. We were taught to take good care of our clothes."

After the mines played out, the amount of merchandise needed up the mountain was not enough to offset the cost of transporting lumber to the valley. Moving the lumber from where it was manufactured to where it was needed was prohibitive. As the *San Francisco Bulletin* noted, the teamsters had no competition and set the freight rates themselves. At a rate of $10 to $12 per thousand board feet delivered, the millmen were at their mercy.

Flume

This situation was intolerable and Leach solved it with a water-filled V-shaped flume. He began its construction in late 1877, worked on it in 1878, and finished it in 1879. "The flume cost $80,000 and is a very great success" (Williams 1887). It is likely that crews worked on the flume at different places with close adherence to grade. At the upper end, thick boards were made at the Diamond Springs mill and for a time these boards, and supports for them, made the flume its best customer. The flume was built in sections, called boxes, each 16 feet long. After a few sections were constructed, water was put in the flume and lumber for the next sections was floated down to where it was needed. This technique saved much time and money, particularly in rough country. The desired grade was 1 inch of fall per box or 27 feet to the mile. This grade could not always be maintained, and at two places along the flume, lumber in it attained a speed of at least 50 miles per hour. The flume was 12 inches wide at the bottom with 30-inch sloping sides, and 48 to 60 inches wide at the water line. It was made of horizontally placed boards with all bracing outside. Additional boards were attached outside at points of extreme wear such as around curves.

The flume directly served the Empire, Deadwood, Woodville, Challenge, and Owl Gulch mills, and indirectly the Beanville operation. The Cottage, Clipper, and Diamond Springs mills were not on the flume. Apparently the Diamond Springs mill was short-lived as a November 16, 1880, entry in an old diary noted "A fearful fire at the Diamond Springs Mill. Leach takes men from Challenge Mill to fight the fire."

The flume received its initial charge of water from Slate Creek, with contributions from other creeks along its route such as Whiskey, Jackass, Deadwood, Owl Gulch, Empire, Hampshire, and Slapjack (McDonald and Lahore 1984). Regulating the amount of water in the flume for its entire length was a tricky business. Some of these streams were small, some large; some yielded large amounts of water just after a storm, and some did not provide storm water until later. Flows tended to be high in late winter and early spring, and much lower in summer and fall. High water in any or all of these streams could destroy the flume. To mitigate storm damage and to regulate flow, a series of headgates and smaller feeder flumes were constructed at several places along the route. The main flume was placed in a ditch wherever possible, and in tunnels and on trestles where necessary.

To get water from Slate Creek, the head of the flume had to be located well above the elevation of the mills. After leaving the Slate Creek canyon, the flume traversed the canyon of the North Fork of the Yuba River and spanned many creeks and gulches, including Owl Gulch Creek. Here a large trestle 166 feet high was necessary (fig. 9).

Regulating the amount of water in the flume for its entire length was a tricky business. Some of these streams were small, some large; some yielded large amounts of water just after a storm, and some did not provide storm water until later. To mitigate storm damage and to regulate flow, a series of headgates and smaller feeder flumes were constructed at several places along the route.

Figure 9—To flume across Owl Gulch creek and canyon, a trestle 166 feet tall was required. Note the mill and typical size of logs in the foreground. Although unknown, a tramway probably carried the lumber to the flume.

The flume then continued into a tunnel, along hillsides, and over many trestles. After it crossed the Alabama Bar Trail to the Yuba River, it contoured along the sheer face of a granite bluff, 500 feet in length. In such areas the flume was anchored to iron pins laboriously drilled into the rock, and ingenuously braced by stout timbers placed against the cliff. Between Hampshire Creek and the crest of the ridge east of Woodville, the terrain was extremely rugged and an intricate series of trestles and a tunnel was needed. Near Empire Creek a long tunnel and a 116-foot trestle had a combined length of one-half mile. Maintaining the proper grade was a rigid requirement because any deviation meant many more feet of costly hillside flume. Such construction was extremely expensive. For this section, the amount of timber required was about 130,000 board feet per mile. On the plus side, the deteriorating mining industry meant that men skilled in boring tunnels in hard rock were available for work at a reasonable wage.

After leaving the crest, the flume traversed much easier terrain, curved around the head of Slapjack Creek, and followed along just below the stage road to the top of the Challenge hill. Here it passed under the road by means of a tunnel. It then plunged down the hill, and crossed the county road where the Catholic church is now. The flume then wound around in back of Brownsville to the top of the Hansonville grade, catapulted down it, and threaded its way through the foothills to its terminus at Moore's Station. Here a planning mill was constructed that employed about 40 men who dressed a million board feet of lumber each year (Williams 1887). A box factory nearby processed about the same amount of lumber. It also was here that all the products from the mountain mills could be loaded into boxcars of the California Northern Railroad for shipment to cities and ports far and wide. Specific ownership of these operations and the people associated with them are largely unknown with one possible exception. George Wolters is mentioned in the *Marysville Appeal* of May 2, 1885, as having a partnership with Andrew Martin Leach that was dissolved by mutual consent. The paper then mentioned that he [Wolters] will "continue the business at Moore's Station," which implies that he either owned or managed one or both of the operations there.

Written accounts of the flume suggested that it was 40 to 80 miles in length, and certainly because of all the turns and twists, was difficult to quantify. However, a more recent endeavor now estimates its length at about 50 miles. In 1976, oldtimer Charles Adams walked the flume location above Challenge and knew of key locations below. He drew the route of the entire flume on U.S. Forest Service topographical maps. Checking of aerial photos and on-the-ground verification by knowledgeable Forest Service employees and other oldtimers interviewed by the authors verify Adam's location with only minor changes.

Written accounts of the flume suggested that it was 40 to 80 miles in length, and certainly because of all the turns and twists, was difficult to quantify. However, a more recent endeavor now estimates its length at about 50 miles.

A large variety of products from wood were placed in the flume, but no logs. The most common articles were various sizes of timbers such as 2 x 4s, 2 x 8s, etc., 16 feet long. Some timbers were 4- to 12-inches-square and up to 24 feet long. The larger pieces often had a little round piece of iron attached to the downward end to smooth passage around the ends of boards that stuck out a little at joints in the flume. One man's job was hauling a wagonload of these devices back to the various mills.

Other products that were placed in the flume were posts, bundles of shakes, railroad ties, and 4-foot lengths of firewood. In 1889, Chinese laborers cut large amounts of wood on Indian Creek, hauled it to the flume, and stacked it. Because maintaining a steady flow of products was based mostly on experience, only Leach employees were allowed to place them in the flume. Settlers clearing land found the flume to their liking: "All the wood that can be supplied is taken at $2.25 per cord at any place along the flume." In 1886, for example, about 6,000 cords were sold. Another "windfall" product from the flume was an occasional trout. One lady who lived near a headgate would catch trout, up to 14 inches long, when it was drained. Apparently the flume was closed during the winter, as were the mills.

The flume was open, and valuable products floating by were vulnerable to theft. Little of this apparently happened. Occasionally a jam or breakout occurred and wood products would spill down the hill. Company workers rarely put this material back into the flume. Men called flume tenders constantly patrolled the flume to look for problems and to ensure that the material was moving along. They would walk the upper side of the ditch, but on trestles a 12- to 18-inch-wide plank served as the walkway. Because some trestles were high aboveground and the narrow planks often were slick with spray or ice, a tender had to have a certain amount of internal fortitude. Near one of the mills, Chinese employees were the patrolmen (Bean 1970).

At strategic places along the flume, cabins well stocked with a stove, bunks, and groceries were built for emergencies. Should a serious problem arise, requiring several days of work and perhaps a crew of men, such foresight served the fluming operation well. Sometimes lumber was flumed at night. If a can full of pebbles hung above the flume kept rattling, the lumber was coming down in good fashion; if it stopped, a patrol up the flume was in order. Each flume tender carried a short-handled curved picaroon (fig. 10), as it was called, to reach in and hook an offending piece of lumber. Around Challenge, the tenders were local citizens. Each patrolled about 4 miles of flume.

Many stories have been written about the "travelers" who journeyed down the flume in "boats." These were nothing more than V-shaped "pig troughs" with

Figure 10—The long-handled, sharp-pointed tools displayed by this crew were called picaroons and used to position lumber and other wood products in the flume.

Because the flume splashed into the millpond at its end, the rider was guaranteed a dunking in cold water. No inebriated traveler was ever known to be anything but stone sober after such a ride.

boards nailed across the top for seats. Occasionally, a celebration in the mountains with a good supply of tarantula juice (slang for cheap whiskey) resulted in a dare for an individual to ride the flume. This must have been a gut-wrenching, hair-raising event as the boat careened around curves, wobbled over the trestles, and plunged down the Challenge and Hansonville grades. Because the flume splashed into the millpond at its end, the rider was guaranteed a dunking in cold water. No inebriated traveler was ever known to be anything but stone sober after such a ride.

Occasionally, a badly wounded person from a remote location in the mountains was placed in a flume boat as a last resort. One hopes that placement was below at least one steep grade and that he was well protected with blankets and oilskins. Shipments of trout and venison, well packed in snow, also made the trip to the valley below.

Leach was well known as forward-thinking, and one of his ideas was to sell the water from his flume to farmers in the valley (Bean 1970). Placing much of the flume in a ditch, for example, was no accident. Indeed, Williams (1887) suggested: "This supply [of water], three hundred miners' inches, is sufficient to irrigate three thousand acres, and all of it will soon be used for that purpose." Try as he might, however, Leach could not justify extending his flume farther into the valley just to sell water.

After Leach went broke and no one was present to maintain the flume or to regulate the amount of water in it, the flume probably deteriorated rapidly, especially in the mountains. However, parts of it must have been present at least until 1908, because in that year, an oldtimer, aged 95, but sound of mind, remembered parking his buggy under one of the trestles because it was nice and cool there. As mentioned earlier, a bustling community called Moore's Station[4] existed at the end of the flume. It was here that Leach's box factory and planning mill existed along with other buildings that supported his operations and housed his workers. In April, 1990, the authors were shown the exact location of Moore's Station. Not a trace remained; no foundations or relicts of any kind could be found. Even the sides of the mill pond were gone. They apparently had been leveled and the land plowed. In 1990, the site was open pastureland.

Railroad

With the advent of the flume, not only could a higher volume of material be shipped to the valley markets, but also products from lower grade logs. These were not low-grade products, but not just "highest" grade as before when only horse-pulled wagons journeyed to the valley. The net effect of this was an increased harvest not only per acre, but also over a larger amount of land. This, in turn lengthened the distance that the logs had to be transported to the mill, and this soon became too costly. Plainly, a more cost-efficient method of transportation was needed.

A narrow-gauged railroad seemed to be the answer. In June 1884, a locomotive and a tender, construction number 7362, were ordered from the Baldwin Locomotive Works by R.E. Woodward for delivery at Moore's Station (McDonald and Lahore 1994). Mr. Woodward was a civil engineer "of more than ordinary ability," noted a newspaper article, and probably responsible for the engineering and construction of the railbed. At some point, this locomotive was named "CHAS KOHLER," a sobriquet that was printed on both sides of the cab just below the windows (fig. 11). Why this name, and who it was, have never been determined. The locomotive was a rod engine, meaning that it had an external horizontal drive system. It had no pilot wheels in front, three sets of large wheels directly under the boiler, and no wheels after the large ones. To trainmen, this designation is termed 0-6-0. The middle pair of the six was "blind" in the sense that it served only to promote stability and distribute weight. The diameter of the cylinders was 8 inches and the stroke 12 inches. The locomotive weighed about 15 tons, which was a

---

[4] The name Moore's Station became obsolete in 1878 when the post office was named Honcut, which is a present-day hamlet close to where Moore's Station was located.

Figure 11—The steam locomotive and loaded flat cars of the Challenge Mill railroad, 1887.

The rolling stock of the Challenge Mill railroad consisted of seven flat cars for hauling logs and lumber.

relatively small engine. It had a fast-steaming boiler and fairly small drive wheels, which meant that it had to have good track, not too much grade, and not too tight curves. Consequently, the railbed and trestles were well constructed with sawed crossties and timbers, as opposed to the round ones, that were traditionally used in logging railroads.

As best as can be determined, and this only by photographic evidence, the rolling stock of the Challenge Mill railroad consisted of seven flat cars for hauling logs and lumber. No boxcars or gondolas (for ballasting the railbed) are known. Long after Leach was gone, a forester found the remains of these flat cars in a gulch near Owl Gulch. "Marysville Foundry 1870" was inscribed on the wheels. Because this was before Leach's railroad, he must have purchased these "flats" second hand.

Construction of the railbed probably began a little before the arrival of the engine in 1884 and continued intermittently as needed for the next 8 years. One oldtimer stated that the "Chinese [from the settlement near Challenge] built the railroad." After the railroad left Challenge, it curved for 2 miles southeastward around Pike County Peak, then forked. One fork extended a short distance above Little Oregon Creek and ended close to where a small settlement called Wrangletown was located. The other fork turned northeastward and continued around the Peak at a 4- to 5-percent grade. Because the track was perpendicular to the drainage pattern, many small bridges, cuts, and fills were needed to maintain this grade. Cuts and fills, pieces of burnt trestles, and in-place railroad ties are visible today.

Wrangletown was a "logging town" and its inhabitants "dirt poor," said an oldtimer. A cutout on the hillside indicated where the principal building was located. Artifacts on three sides of the cutout included many lead-soldered cans, old shoes, broken ax heads, and shards of broken Chinese rice bowls and bottles. Enough of the broken bottles were left to categorize them as whiskey, chutney, spice, and medicine. All dated to the late 19th century. Several pieces of early logging machinery and a large iron rim for a wooden wagon wheel were deposited along the hillside and near the stream bottom below. The town was not Chinese, said the oldtimer, and poor White folks could have utilized the cheaper oriental crockery. Judging from the small amount of one age of cans and bottles (the time of the railroad), Wrangletown was short-lived.

By 1887, the rails had penetrated for another 2½ miles into the forest to Beanville Creek, where a new, but smaller, sawmill and supporting structures were constructed. The railroad now switched from hauling logs to the mill to hauling lumber to the flume (fig. 12). A portable, steam-driven donkey engine snaked at least some of the logs out of ravines to a landing (fig. 13), where the oxen could then move them to the mill. The Beanville mill operated from 1888 to 1892. Eventually, the railroad extended across Beanville Creek, over to Indian Creek, and up it for a short distance. It never crossed Indian Creek. The total trackage from Challenge to its farthest point was about 6 miles.

Figure 12—Numerous cuts and fills were needed to maintain the rail grade from the Beanville mill to the Challenge flume.

Figure 13—This little, wood-burning, steam donkey engine and crew snaked logs out of the woods enroute to the Beanville Mill in the early 1890s.

Beanville was a small settlement connected to Challenge by rail and probably by road. We know it existed in 1889 and 1890. The sawmill shut down during the winter and the people went elsewhere. A cutout in the hillside pinpointed the location of the boiler and probably of the mill itself. A plethora of old bricks, saw teeth, and square nails nearby support this contention. Today, a large decomposing sawdust pile, well dotted with ferns, bleeding hearts, and buttercups cascades down the hill into Beanville Creek. Artifacts of glass and metal along the old railroad right-of-way leading to the mill verify at least temporary living quarters for the mill workers.

Speaking of a sawdust pile, it was common practice in those days for a sawmill to "run their sawdust" by means of a small water-filled flume beneath the headsaw. The water carried off the sawdust downhill and deposited it into what often became a huge pile. At one of Leach's mills, an enterprising fellow tunneled into the pile, hauled in blocks of ice, and had a ready-made refrigerator there for years. Of course, cold drinks could then be supplied to thirsty passersby for a small remittance.

By 1892, Leach again needed more timber. He already owned a tract of land containing a large amount of superb sugar pine about 8 miles above Challenge in the Owl Gulch area. And his flume was nearby. Here he constructed a sawmill of the same name. He also needed his railroad to move the logs to the mill, so he built a short railbed there that was about 3/4 of a mile long. Moving the mill machinery, engine, and flat cars uphill to this location was no easy task. Leach apparently constructed a road to Owl Gulch, purchased a wood-burning, iron-wheeled road engine (fig. 14), and somehow transported everything, together or in pieces, to the site. The Owl Gulch mill operated until 1894.

Figure 14—Road engine and empty log truck in front of Leach's home at Challenge Mills in 1892.

The lumbering empire of Andrew Martin Leach probably peaked in 1886. Although the Diamond Springs mill had burned in 1880 and the Cottage mill had closed, the remaining mills were producing well and the flume was mostly paid for. The Woodville and Challenge mills alone were producing about 8 million board feet annually. A celebration was called for and what better way to celebrate than with a train ride (fig. 15).

Gus Batt was about 17 and suffering with asthma in 1876. His doctor advised him to go to California and settle in a mountain town with pure air. Gus had to be carried on a stretcher to a train in Buffalo, New York, bound for California. We don't know how he happened to choose Yuba County, California, but he settled in Brownsville where his health began to improve. His first job was cutting cordwood. He eventually went to work for Leach, progressed to being woods boss, and then to superintendent at the Challenge mill.

The Empire mill possibly was unique in three respects. The first was that the mill was located below the flume and a tramway was constructed to raise the lumber to it. The second was that Leach built a skidway of peeled logs up Empire Creek for a mile or more and skidded peeled logs down it to the mill. A correspon-

Figure 15—Never one to miss an opportunity for a little favorable public relations, Andrew Martin Leach decked out his train in 1886, probably for a Fourth-of-July celebration.

After 1886 a series of disasters hit. "Leach's mill at Challenge, Yuba County, burned, completely destroying (also) about half a million feet of lumber. Six months later, the planning mill, adjacent box factory, and a loaded boxcar at Moore's Station also were destroyed by fire.

dent remarked that there was still a big pile of rotten bark on the creek where the skidway started. The third respect was that production lasted longer at this mill than any other of Leach's original mills. It closed in 1894.

After 1886 a series of disasters hit. According to an article in a widely circulated trade journal of the time, *Pacific Coast Wood and Iron* (1887): "Leach's mill at Challenge, Yuba County, burned, completely destroying (also) about half a million feet of lumber. The loss will run into the hundred thousands. Not more than $5,000 insurance is on the entire property." Six months later, the planning mill, adjacent box factory, and a loaded boxcar at Moore's Station also were destroyed by fire. Most of the lumber piles were saved, however, by using water from the pond at the base of the flume. Several weeks later, the Woodville mill also was consumed by fire. Even the weather conspired against Leach. The winter of 1889 was termed the "big snow" by several oldtimers, with the snowpack being 12 feet deep on level ground at Woodville and 20 feet deep at higher elevations. Indeed, tunnels were dug to doors and windows of some homes and businesses for egress and light. Worst of all, the big snow took out whole sections of the flume, usually in the most inaccessible and most expensive places to repair. The Deadwood mill ceased to function about this time as well.

At this point, his empire was crumbling, but Leach continued on. The Beanville mill and extension of operations to Indian Creek and later to the Owl Gulch area are witness to his persistence. Financing to repair the flume, build the new mills, and keep operations going was vital. Some money was realized as deeds from the county recorder's office show that several parcels of land were sold in 1889 and 1890. Nevertheless, Leach must have braved the financial jungles of San Francisco and borrowed heavily at this time. The winter of 1890 again was severe, and the newspaper *Daily Mercury* of Oroville, California noted "This has been a disastrous season for sawmills in the mountains. The rains have kept the ground so soft that it is impossible to haul. The Challenge mills have been idle most of the time."

Ever optimistic, Leach talked of extending his flume farther down the Feather River, forming a new company, and building two mills. However, no record exists of this ever happening. To make matters worse, the depression of 1893 was very bad. Another article in the *Pacific Coast Wood and Iron* (1893) stated: "The lumber interest in California looks black. The depression in general business has affected the entire trade and millmen are going slow. Some mills have shut down and other mills are working only part time. The only thing for lumbermen to do is wait. The present state of affairs cannot last always, and soon brighter times may be expected." However, brighter times did not emerge, and sometime in 1894, Levi and Greenwald of San Francisco closed the books and took over all of Leach's holdings on the ridge, even his house.

When asked about the Leach insolvency, several oldtimers seemed philosophical about it. Almost all lumber mills eventually go broke, one said. Another remarked that "Leach did more for this part of the northern Sierra than any other."

Some Aspects of Life in Challenge

Stories of the inhabitants of Challenge Mills are always poignant, sometimes happy or sad, and at times fulfilling or giving evidence of a struggle. For good times, one lady noted that "not much time was spent away from home. In the winter evenings, we often would sit around the fireplace and our father would read to us. Mother and the girls did a lot of sewing and crocheting. Once in a while, we, or some of the neighbors, had parties with singing, dancing, games, and outdoor get-togethers (fig. 16). This and an occasional school function were about all the entertainments we had in those days. We also had baseball and horse-shoe throwing for men and boys in the summer and skiing and sledding in the winter." An example of winter fun was told by a fellow, who as a child would build homemade skis out of old barrel staves. These were remarkably unstable and a tumble in the snow often resulted.

Figure 16—Young people, all dressed up in their Sunday best, at Lover's Leap near Challenge in 1914 from left include Gus Kelly, Arta Blodgett, Martin Costa, Bob Roy, Mrs. Blodgett, her family, Viola Kelly, Gertrude Mellon, Marie Mellon, and Phil Kelly.

Soon, the skis evolved to sleds made of several barrel staves. If the hill was steep, a backstop of tree limbs would be built at the lower end to make a sort of cushion. Crashing into that was part of the fun. Of course, autumn was the time of harvest and most everyone had a garden and orchard. In the later part of October, entire families would take their lunch and visit their orchard in a horse-drawn wagon. "We would spend the whole day picking and packing apples and playing. We children also picked berries and had a lot of fun." Christmas time was one of great joy for the family. Most families had a Christmas tree decorated with popcorn and paper chains.

For tough times, another correspondent stated: "Mother became janitor for the school and my oldest sister and I were her helpers. We used to beat the chalk erasers against the old flag pole and dust out the desks. Mother's pay was a few dollars a month and a sack of flour. She also baked bread for the miners and washed their clothes using an old wash board. Clothes were pressed with an iron kept hot on the wood stove. The children's job was to keep the wood box full, and to pick berries and work in many ways."

The way of life at Challenge during the 1875 to 1915 period is told no better than to portray the Kelly family and in particular some thoughts of Edna (Kelly) Heenan (fig. 17). The Kelly family moved to Challenge in 1888 from Brush Creek,

Figure 17—Edna Kelly in 1909 at age 18.

Butte County, and lived in two cabins joined by a breezeway (fig. 18). One cabin was mostly bedrooms. There were six kids in the family; four boys and two girls. All were born at Challenge except the oldest, Albert. Edna Kelly was one of the girls. Her story was different from that of most children at Challenge because she went to college. Her brother, Albert, worked for the Forest Service (U.S. Department of Agriculture) and the money he earned helped put her through teachers college. Edna attended school in San Francisco and after becoming a teacher taught school in several places, including Marysville and Live Oak. She married well, had children who were successful in business, and lived a long, full life.

Figure 18—The Kelly family and home at Challenge, circa 1890. In the front row are Viola, Augustine, Philip, and Ellen (Feeney) Kelly and in the back row are Gus, Albert, Edna, and Ernest. The family lived in one part and slept in the other. The bedroom part was not heated, and long-johns were standard bedtime garb in winter.

Because money was short, the shoes were worn long after the children's feet had outgrown them. "That is the reason I have bunions now. If the shoes squeaked, that was the nice part of it. As I went up the isle to the blackboard at school, they squeaked, and everyone knew I had shoes."

Edna told us: "We always had an immense garden on a whole acre of ground where we grew all kinds of produce, including winter vegetables. My mother used to can all of our vegetables and meat. She canned everything for the winter because there wasn't much money coming in around that time. It was kind of tough picking for all of us. My father had a cow and raised hogs. He would butcher them and put the meat down as salt pork. He smoked the hams in the smokehouse. We also had lots of eggs. We didn't lack for anything to eat, and I can't say that we really suffered any. It was the money that came in that was scarce." Indeed, one individual recalled being in the Challenge store in the winter and observing a client purchasing several sacks of groceries. When it was time to pay, not a word was said; he simply tapped the cuff of his jacket. "On the cuff" was how many families got through the winter. For most, it was a badge of honor to pay the bill as soon as a paycheck was coming in. This process of borrowing and paying back often was repeated year after year.

Edna attended school at Challenge and remarked that she had one change of clothes in her wardrobe. Her mother would buy bolts of material at the store and sit up nights sewing clothes for the two girls. Her mother and father had shoes, as did the girls in the family. When there wasn't any rain or snow, her brothers went to school barefoot. Her shoes came from the catalog, and although they didn't fit very well, she was proud of them. Because money was short, the shoes were worn long after the children's feet had outgrown them. "That is the reason I have bunions now. If the shoes squeaked, that was the nice part of it. As I went up the isle to the blackboard at school, they squeaked, and everyone knew I had shoes."

As to social decorum, Edna noted: "We had long dresses in those days with white underskirts. They tended to drag in the dust, but we had soft water up here and they came out nice and clean after washing. I remember my grandmother telling my mother that the girls should wear dresses longer. We weren't allowed to sneak around much like the kids do now. My father never allowed me to go out alone with anyone even when I was up all night going to the dances. Sometimes he even told me who I couldn't dance with, and when I came back he would ask me. I always told him the truth. I had to be very, very careful. My oldest brother looked after me. If anybody danced with me too often he was told. He got into a big scrap one night because of that. I remember the big Fourth-of-July celebration at Wood-ville very well. It was at that dance that they brought me the letter that I had passed the teachers examination. Did I ever celebrate."

There were no churches in Challenge at the time. A Catholic priest would go to the different houses and have services there. "He came to our home quite often. Mother would sit on our beds at night and teach all six of us our prayers. That was where we learned them. Father Toumey was one priest that I remember. He was on his way to Challenge one winter evening and had to cross Dry Creek. It was very swift and his horse and buggy was swept away and he was drowned."

The Forest Service arrived in the Challenge area about 1908, first as part of the Tahoe National Forest and then as a component of the Plumas National Forest. The Forest Service's main job was to protect the forest from fire and its best known presence was the lookout near the top of a pine tree (fig. 19) on the summit of Pike County Peak. The platform for the observer was none too large, and rather flimsy. Observers (lookouts) were required to climb up and check for smoke several times a day, and if any was spotted, they had to hike to the spot and put out the fire (Moss-inger 2006). Henry Foss was the lookout there for 15 years. One elderly lady and a dear friend would flash him with a looking glass at noon every day to let him know that the older lady was all right. One oldtimer remarked that he was "scared spit-less" up there. Other Forest Service employees at Challenge during this period were Elmer Gleason, Charlie LaValle, and William Hayes.

When asked, one oldtimer could not remember any hangings or shoot-outs in Challenge. "There were individual shootings aplenty however. Generally the sheriffs were pretty good guys. When a man was shot, the sheriff would come up and investigate. He would ask around and if told the guy was a no-good s.o.b. and deserved to be shot, he'd write down 'shot by another while shooting in self defense,

The Forest Service arrived in the Challenge area about 1908. The Forest Service's main job was to protect the forest from fire and its best known presence was the lookout near the top of a pine tree on the summit of Pike County Peak. The platform for the observer was none too large, and rather flimsy. One oldtimer remarked that he was "scared spitless" up there.

Figure 19—U.S. Forest Service lookout on top of Pike County Peak in 1909.

investigation closed.' However, if the man did not deserve to be shot, the shooter went rather quickly and decisively to jail."

Like today, the cold was the most common illness followed by appendicitis, heart attacks, and kidney malfunction. Pneumonia often followed a cold, as the many miners in the hills breathed a toxic mix of rock dust, powder smoke, and bad air. Many deaths simply were recorded as "cause unknown."

In the smaller towns and mining camps, doctors were unavailable. Treatment was by family and friends and often surprisingly effective. Medicines tended to be homemade with the most common elements being sulfur and syrup. A cold was universally treated by greasing one's chest with turpentine and lard and then wrapping it with a big flannel cloth. Being "mustarded" was another treatment. A raw potato in your pocket was good for rheumatism. Pain from a bad cavity in a tooth was alleviated with a piece of cotton swabbed with carbolic acid. Typically, only the larger towns had a doctor. If someone was sick, a friend or relative would travel to a town that had a doctor, describe the symptoms, and get a bottle of medicine. If an emergency, the doctor would travel to the victim. However, in the winter, a trip on snowshoes often was necessary.

Sometime in 1894, one oldtimer sadly remembered that it was about this time that typhoid fever became rampant and several people died. "Typhoid continued to stalk the countryside and no one knew when he might be the next victim." Tuberculosis also was common throughout the area. There was a County Hospital located in Marysville for the indigent. County aid was $5 per month. "Many an old prospector lived on it," said one fellow.

The California legislature offered premiums as an incentive to produce rosin turpentine from pine trees.

The Town of Challenge

Little is known about Challenge Mills as a town before the coming of Andrew Martin Leach. Undoubtedly, a few structures were present to support the early-day sawmill, as well as those of miners, farmers, and other minor industries. A stage-stop also must have been present.

By the 1860s, mining for gold in the small creeks around Challenge was depleted, but a new industry emerged. This was the gathering of sap from pine trees for the manufacture of rosin and turpentine. The Civil War had cut off the supply of these products to the North (Bancroft 1890), and the California legislature offered premiums as an incentive to produce them. J.W. Jacobson of Marysville gained the first incentive, and in 1864 fully 350,000 pounds of crude pitch were collected. His three distilleries made over 7,000 gallons of turpentine and 1,150 barrels of rosin. Each tree yielded about 3 gallons of crude. Cronise (1868) stated that "The home-made article is equal to the imported, and could be produced in almost any quantity and at less price than the Eastern were it not for the cost of freight from the interior to San Francisco, the central market." The cessation of war virtually ended this endeavor. A few large pines with almost healed-over scars can still be seen in the forest near Challenge today (fig. 20).

Plentiful sunshine, abundant rain, and good soil suggested that the Challenge area would be a good area for farming. The 1886 land survey denoted "cultivated"

Figure 20—A cat-face scar from turpentine extraction on a large ponderosa pine tree on the Challenge Experimental Forest in 1980.

land surrounding Challenge and to extend south and east of it about three forths of a mile. All was described as "being won from the forest." Cultivated land, however, must have included pasture and grazing land as well as orchards and small fields of oats and barley. One oldtimer mentioned that a grist mill was located below a small waterfall on Dry Creek in the experimental forest, but only a few bricks and pieces of crockery are all that remain today.

As Leach's operations became established and grew, new houses and businesses were built in Challenge. All were constructed of wood because it was plentiful and cheap. From 1875 to 1887, Challenge was a vigorous, bustling, expanding town with an aura of unbridled optimism. Most of the homes in Challenge were constructed during this time of maximum prosperity and were reasonably well made and furnished. Many homes had several owners, and those denoted on the schematic (fig. 21) are named for the family that lived there either first or the longest. In a few instances, the authors knew a house was present in a given location but received no information as to the owner. Of course, most homes also had one or more outbuildings like the ubiquitous outhouse, barns for livestock, sheds for tools, and root cellars for potatoes, tuberous vegetables, and apples. Most businesses in Challenge arose after the sawmill burned and Leach's empire crumbled.

As Leach's operations became established and grew, new houses and businesses were built in Challenge. All were constructed of wood because it was plentiful and cheap. From 1875 to 1887, Challenge was a vigorous, bustling, expanding town with an aura of unbridled optimism.

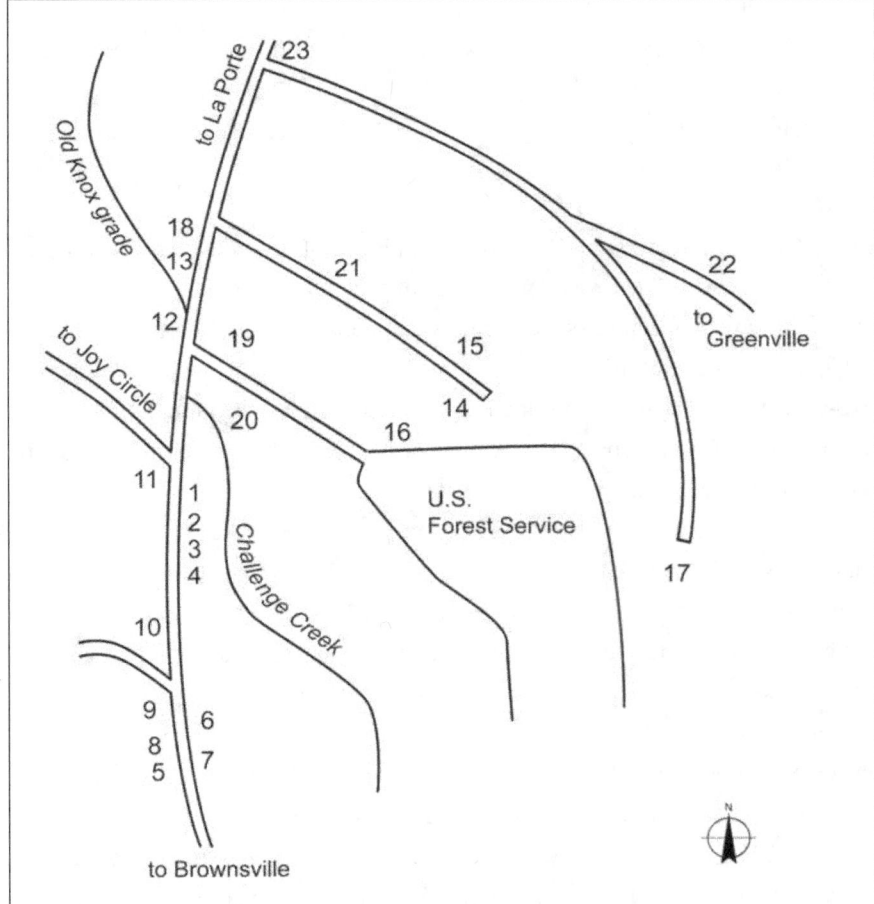

Figure 21—Schematic of homes and businesses in Challenge in 1914. Houses: 1–Henry South, 3–no information, 9–Ashburn, 10–Cartland, 11–no information, 12–Wilder, 13–Willey, 14–Leach, 15–Mellon, 16–Pike, 17–Costa, 18–Kelly, 19–Pieratt, 20–Mulock, 23–Clemons.

Below is a numbered listing of the homes, businesses, and other prominent structures in Challenge in the 1886 to 1890 era. Most are long gone with numbers 1, 2, 10, 13, 14, and 20 remaining. Of these, most are abandoned. More description and stories of some of them follow in the same order.

Number	Description	Number	Description
1	House (Henry South)	13	House (Willey)
2	Store (Hendricks)	14	House (Leach)
3	House	15	House (Mellon)
4	Store (H. Clemons)	16	House (Pike)
5	Small barn	17	House (Costa)
6	Blacksmith shop	18	House (Kelly)
7	Large barn	19	House (Pieratt)
8	Hotel	20	House (Mulock)
9	House, (Ashburn)	21	Boarding house (Leach)
10	House (Cartland)	22	School
11	House	23	House (Clemons
12	House (Wilder)		

Number 1. Henry South was a long-time employee of Leach who worked in the woods and at the mill. He drove an ox team and may have been one of the early engineers on the railroad. Later, Isaac Ryant was an engineer on the railroad that ran from Challenge to Beanville.

Number 2. After Leach went broke, there were two relatively small stores in Challenge. Frank and Nell Hendricks had a grocery store, which after many modifications and additions became the Challenge store. It closed in 2010.

Number 3. No history.

Number 4. Belle and Henry Clemons had a general store at this location, where they sold a general line of hardware and merchandise. One of the Clemons was described as a good dresser and a good talker. He spent most of his time in the store playing poker with his pals. He was a real good poker player, said one fellow rather wistfully.

Number 5. At one time, two barns of note existed in Challenge. This, the smaller one, was next to the hotel and served as the stage barn.

Number 6. Blacksmith shop operated by Henry Coupe. Numerous horse and ox shoes, square nails, and pieces of heavy metal were found nearby. Henry logged and did timber work for Leach for several years. One day, Henry and several of his friends were standing around and discussing the weather, news, and current events. Business was slow, so out came the bottle, and they all had a few. Henry liked cigars, and at one point put one in his mouth, lighted end first. It was said that he never even flinched, laid the cigar down, spit out the ashes, remarked that he had burned his blankety-blank tongue, turned around, and walked out. His buddies howled with laughter and he never did live it down.

Number 7. This large barn (fig. 22) was used by the many teamsters who traveled the Challenge roadway. It had doors at both ends and thus was easy to drive through. Barns were important in the old days as horses were the sole link with the outside world. Consequently, the animals were well kept and well fed. The barns were filled with oats, barley, hay, and straw in the fall. It was a big and expensive job to put away feed for the animals. It also was here that the kids, sitting on the corral fences, and hearing the men when they changed horses, learned how to cuss.

Figure 22—This large barn at Challenge served commerce in the area for many years.

Number 8. The big 2-story Challenge Hotel was built in 1886 by J.W. and Susan Ribble at a cost of $4,000 to $5,000. They also lived in it. Doctor J.J. Van Male bought the hotel in 1909-1910 for $1,800 (fig. 23). It burned on November 12, 1914. The hotel had 16 rooms, described as "nice" with an even nicer bar, said one fellow. Drinks were two for a quarter, a bottle of whiskey cost one dollar, and gin traded hands at 75 cents a fifth. Most rooms had a bed, a wash stand with bowl and pitcher, a drinking water pitcher, soap dish, and of course a chamberpot.

Figure 23—As the center for local social life, the Challenge Hotel was built by J.W. Ribble in 1886 and served the community until November 11, 1914, when it burned to the ground. The automobile is a 1914 Henderson, Model 54, roadster.

Saturday was bath night. One individual remarked "There must have been quite a scramble for everyone to get a bath that night.

A person had to have either lamps or candles for lighting. The lamps burned kerosene and they constantly had to be filled and cleaned. Almost all hotels had one big galvanized bath tub, and Saturday was bath night. One individual remarked "There must have been quite a scramble for everyone to get a bath that night. All water would have to be heated and carried." There were large tanks for water on the cook stove in the kitchen.

Each town along the road had a big dance at least once a year. Challenge had the New Year's dance; Forbestown—Christmas; Brownville—Thanksgiving; Woodville—Fourth of July. The dances started on Saturday and wouldn't end until all hours Sunday night. For some, going home was painful because of too much strong drink, but Monday was a work day, so home they went. Music was by old-time fiddlers and pianists; sometimes with a cornet or banjo. Two-steps, quadrilles, waltzes, and an occasional polka were offered. Of course, good food and the nice bar enhanced the celebration. The Challenge Hotel would actively advertise its big dance with posters put up near and far. People would come from miles around and dance until daylight the next morning in the big dormitory upstairs. We have a conflict here, as one correspondent mentioned that several bedrooms were present upstairs in the hotel.

Shortly after the hotel burned, the first permanent physician in Challenge, Doctor J.J. Van Male (fig. 24), built his home where it had been. "Doc" Van Male graduated from the California Medical College in December 1887 with the degree of M.D., and practiced his profession in various locations in San Francisco and northern California before moving to Challenge in 1897. Doc was head of the County Hospital in Yuba City before coming to Challenge. He was the only doctor in the area and a rather colorful character.

Doc had a sense of humor: One oldtimer needed a medical exam and the test included looking at his eyes, ears, etc. Doc had a big old watch that sounded like a threshing machine. The story goes that he held it a few feet from the man's ear and said: "Can you hear that?" After an affirmative, he kept backing away asking all the time: "Can you hear that?" Finally, he went clear into the next room and asked again. When the answer was "yes," he came out and said: "You're a dam--d liar."

Doc had a rig in the ceiling with pulleys that had hand grips. It came down and had a leather collar to put around his neck. He would raise that up and those hand grips would stretch his spine. Another time he was observed coming from his house grumbling and cussing a little: "The woman just had another 'young-un' and hasn't paid the $5.00 she owed from the last."

One day in November 1911, another correspondent had a badly cut hand, and was brought to Doc Van Male, who stitched it up. "He used one heck of a big needle; just like the one they use to sew sacks shut. One man had to hold me down while the sewing was done." This operation must have been successful, because the hand was good for another 60 years. Another fellow broke a finger. Doc put some stinky powdered medicine on it, wrapped it up, and returned 2 weeks later to remove the bandage. It was all healed.

In general, the folks at Challenge got along pretty well, but an occasional dispute arose: "Complaint has again been made to the office of District Attorney E. Ray Manwell by Dr. J.J. Van Male of Challenge regarding the alleged maintenance of a nuisance in the freedom allowed hogs by F.C. Cuddeback, a neighbor of the complainant. Several months ago a similar complaint was lodged by Van Male resulting in an investigation and arrest of Cuddeback for a violation of the law in allowing his hogs to pollute a stream of water used for drinking purposes. The case was dismissed after Cuddeback agreed to remedy the condition. Van Male now complains that his neighbor has a larger band of hogs than ever and that he is much annoyed. Manwell will endeavor to settle the dispute through diplomacy."

Doc Van Male also served residents in the small towns above Challenge whom he would visit via horse and buggy. Summertime charges ranged from $3.50 to $5.00 per visit and included medicines or pills. Wintertime was much different, and

Figure 24—Doctor Van Male and wife, circa 1900.

a trip on snowshoes cost several times more money. This was not surprising as such trips often took several days and were much more risky, given the possibility of severe winter storms, fallen trees, and avalanches.

Visits by dentists and eye doctors also tended to be seasonal. Care was given only in the summer months when a traveling dentist or optician would come to town and open temporary offices in the Challenge Hotel.

Number 9. In July 1915, C.E. Ashburn and wife turned their private home (fig. 25) into a hotel for a short time.

Figure 25—Ashburn house, circa 1914.

Between the Ashburn and Cartland houses was a building occupied at one time by the Order of the Owls, which was a fraternal organization. In later years, it was known for its dances and wild parties. We did not denote it on the schematic because we were not sure where the original "Owl's Nest" was located, nor if it was in our time period.

Number 10. Known at one time as the Gephart or Cartland house (fig. 26), but no other history known.

Number 11. No history.

Number 12. Could have been called the Blodgett house. Later owned by Hugh Wilder. In 1910, he was an old white-haired man and a noted musician who could play the piano, violin, and cornet.

Figure 26—Nestled among the incense-cedar and locust trees, the Cartland house overlooks the Marysville-La Porte highway.

Mr. Mellon was a good politician. In an election year, he would visit certain areas and give the people there a job working on the roads. He helped me out more than once to get a job on the road. The pay was $2 a day. I worked for him many a time and my brothers did also.

Number 13. Aileen M. Willey (fig. 27) and mother were agents for the telephone exchange in Challenge beginning in 1904. The switch board was located in the Willey house. Aileen also had the Post Office in 1909 and for many years afterward.

Number 14. Andrew Martin Leach house (fig. 28). This large two-story house was described as well made with fine siding, and plastered and beautifully appointed inside. After Leach, several families lived here over the years. One family was Doctor and Mrs. S.C. Gearhart who practiced medicine in the area after 1910. He was highly regarded, said one correspondent.

Number 15. First known as the Pratt house, and then the home of William J. Mellon (fig. 29). Henry S. Pratt was the head sawyer for Leach for many years.

Mr. Mellon moved from Butte County to Challenge in 1889 where he engaged in lumbering and mining. In February 1895, Mr. Mellon was nominated on the Democratic ticket as county supervisor of the fifth district of Yuba County and took the oath of office in March 1895 (fig. 30). He served as county supervisor from 1895 to 1938, being elected every 4 years. Mr. Mellon was described "as a pleasant and capable supervisor. He had an old sorrel horse that was as old as he was. He loved that horse. He also was described as someone who was a nice dresser, wore kid gloves, and was always sober. He never drank. He also was a good politician. In an

Figure 27—Willey house.

Figure 28—Leach house, 1914.

election year, he would visit certain areas and give the people there a job working on the roads. He helped me out more than once to get a job on the road. The pay was $2 a day. I worked for him many a time and my brothers did also. Everybody around, he gave them all work. We hauled gravel on the road. When asked if he voted for Mr. Mellon, the answer with a smile was yes, more than once. When not

Figure 29—Pratt house and then home of William J. Mellon.

Figure 30—Yuba County Board of Supervisors, 1895. Mr. Mellon is at far left, front row.

an election year, local folks would say: road bad, big holes. Mr. Mellon would shake his head and say: "We don't have any money—just have to get by with the roads that we have."

Number 16. This house was described as large, rectangular, and surounded by a white picket fence, fruit trees, and flowers. It was built in 1883 and probably lived in by George Wolters and family (Mossinger 2006). After 1885, it was known as the Pike house where a big family with two boys and several girls resided. It was built with square nails and had a porch all around that was good for sleeping during the summer

Number 17. The Costa family were pioneers in the Challenge area and at least one member lived here.

Number 18. The Kelly family suffered from at least one burned home, but lived here the latest. More on the family was told earlier by Edna (Kelly) Heenan.

Number 19. Known as the Pieratt House, but no other history is known.

Number 20. Original owners unknown, but lived in for many years by Mr. and Mrs. Mulock.

Number 21. Leach boarding house.

Number 22. School house. The Challenge school began in 1881 and operated for 8 months during the winter. It had only one room with one teacher for 25 to 45 pupils from first grade to 10th grade (fig. 31). For some children, the school was 2 or 3 miles away. "We didn't mind walking a few miles in those days," said one young fellow. There was one row of single desks and two rows of double desks. The subjects were much like those of today: arithmetic, English, penmanship, geography, and history. Some of the teacher's names were Ida Ruff, Ben DeVore, Elsie Pottle, George Johnson, and Mabel Kumle (fig. 32). One lady told of her brother attending the Challenge school: "It was a very good school and he had no trouble when he attended schools elsewhere." This extended to college as well.

> The Challenge school began in 1881 and operated for 8 months during the winter. It had only one room with one teacher for 25 to 45 pupils from first grade to 10th grade. For some children, the school was 2 or 3 miles away. "We didn't mind walking a few miles in those days," said one young fellow.

Figure 31—Children at the Challenge School. Note the bare feet of the two boys in the center of the picture.

Figure 32—A native of nearby Brownsville, Mabel Kumle taught school at Challenge from 1906 to 1909 and was featured on the cover of the graduation program in 1907.

Number 23. Mrs. Addie Clemons had a little, square, white house near the intersection of the present-day La Porte and Greenville roads. Her children Henry, Dave, Fred, Nell and another daughter lived there. Mrs. Clemons lived in this house at the same time Nell (Mrs. Hendricks) and her husband, Frank, had the Challenge store. Dave Clemons used to haul their provisions out of Marysville with a two-horse wagon.

Less than a mile north of Challenge was a gold mine, called the "Horseshoe." It was located by Fred Clemons in 1908–09 and owned by him for several years. Initially, he took some good gold out of the mine, and built a small stamp mill nearby to crush the ore and a cyanide mill to extract the gold from it. Later, it became tough going because the rock was faulted. It would be good rock for one foot and bad the next. Many a boy would go up to the mine for target shooting on warm afternoons when the rattlesnakes were sunning themselves on the rocks. It was quite common to see a fellow coming down the trail with 18 or 20 snakes, said one lady. After one close encounter, Earnest Kelly (fig. 33) and some friends dynamited the den. They counted over 300 dead snakes after the blast; they were all over; even hanging from the trees.

Figure 33—Earnest Kelly on the trail to the Horseshoe gold mine.

Two important businesses in Challenge were the Post Office and the Telephone Exchange. These were not given a number because they were located in several homes or buildings over the years.

Before it had a Post Office, mail for Challenge Mills could be collected at the Post Office in Brownsville to the south or at Clipper Mills, Butte County, to the north. The Challenge, Yuba County Post Office was established on April 29, 1895 (General Services Administration 1975), with its location being in the homes of several people. Postmasters were Elijah B. Sparks 1895, Mrs. Susan E. Ribbel 1899, Charles E. Congrave 1903, Eunice Reed 1905, and Aileen M. Willey 1909. In 1897, some people that had gotten mail at Brownsville continued to do so even after the Post Office at Challenge came into being.

With the sawmills gone, employment was hard to find, and most men worked at anything that they could get. They would even leave their families if the only work available was out of town. Money was always scarce, and in winter was even harder to come by.

Telephone service at Challenge was officially opened on February 28, 1906, but the town got its first telephone a few years before the turn of the century. This was a long-distance public pay station. An 1897 telephone directory showed J. W. Ribbel as agent for the line. One fellow talked to a friend through the telephone and remarked that this was his "first experience in such witchery."

In 1902, oldtimer Alex Moran said: "I worked for the Pacific Electric Company for some time. In the early days, the telephone line followed the county roads. They would buy poles from anybody that could secure them, dig the holes, put up a bracket for the insulator, and string just one wire. They would put a telephone here and there, three or four miles apart. Somebody would take charge of it and kind of handle it. People would come and phone. Of course, it was a ground-and-return system and was quite noisy and awfully hard to carry on a conversation. They had many calls from different bells along the line like the long-short-long, two longs and a short, and all that kind of stuff. They would be ringing those. People that wanted to find out what the news was would get on the line. Pretty soon you couldn't hear anything with too many people on to hear what the news was."

Many humorous stories were told on how to get chronic listeners off the line. Sometimes an outrageous story would be told to a listener who was suspected of being on the line for hours. When the tale was repeated, the listener was then known and rather strongly told to keep off the line henceforth.

Moran continued "The poles didn't last but a few years. Then they had to stub them to keep them holding the wire up. A hole was dug beside the pole and a heart-cedar post about 7 to 7 ½ feet long was planted there. Then a bolt was put through and a couple strands of wire were wrapped around the pole and the stub." A few of these stubs can be seen along the Marysville-La Porte highway today.

The Decline

With the sawmills gone, employment was hard to find, and most men worked at anything that they could get. They would even leave their families if the only work available was out of town. Money was always scarce, and in winter was even harder to come by. A few businesses took the place of Leach's store and blacksmith shop, and a smaller sawmill was constructed in the Challenge area after 1915. Few, if any, new homes were built.

The population also began to decline: an oldtimer remarked "One by one, they (the miners) started dying off. Many a night I spent sitting up with them 'till they died. The men here would bathe and shave them and put them in their best clothes. Someone else would take a wagon over to Brownsville where the general store had a drug department, and get a coffin. There was a cemetery there and that is where most of the people from Challenge were buried. Everybody generally turned out when there was a funeral and someone would read the Book. It was a very simple life."

Hunting and trapping helped to supplement food and meager incomes. Both were commonplace. One fellow noted "In those days there were no laws governing hunting and there was no such thing as limits or closed seasons. We needed meat, especially in the winter, and would kill deer, squirrels, and other small game. We did not hunt unless we needed the meat. If someone was lucky, he might kill a couple of deer and then go around to a neighbor and offer a hind quarter. Upon acceptance, dinner often was offered in the next few days. That's the way it was with neighbors."

One fellow had a favorite bear story: It seems like some fellows killed a deer, wrapped it in an old mattress, and placed it in part of a fallen-down cellar. That evening a bear came along and eloped with the deer, mattress and all. The next morning one fellow followed the bear tracks into the woods until he came upon the mattress lying against some brush. Upon poking the mattress, some loud grunts ensued and out came a thoroughly aroused bear. After a moment of sheer fright, the fellow went one way and the bear the other—both in record time.

Before 1900, there was good trapping around Challenge for coons, civet cats, foxes, coyotes, and small game. Some animals were used for food and their pelts for useful items around the house. Sometimes a pelt could be sold for a bit of income.

After going broke, Leach apparently stayed in the Challenge area for a short time, trying to square-up with his employees. For many, this meant payment in goods from the company store or even assigning them a small piece of land. Another oldtimer's father was given a white horse named "Flora," 25 years old, to repay a loan. Soon after, the two remaining mills (fig. 34), locomotive, track, and flume were simply abandoned. In 1899, one oldtimer, then a boy, remembered the locomotive and tender, and especially the bronze bell. Another old timer remarked: "I remember seeing the locomotive when I was quite small. My uncle hauled it out from Owl Gulch with eight horses and a deadax (meaning no springs) wagon minus the wheels. He hauled it to Marysville and it was shipped someplace. This was about 1902. The brass bell was still on it." Apparently the wheels of the locomotive were transported in a separate wagon. The flatcars simply disappeared, but were noticed from time to time in the Owl Gulch area by local fishermen. In 1943, they were salvaged as scrap to support World War II. In the 1920s, an engine with the same wheel configuration turned up near San Rafael, in the San Francisco bay area. It apparently had been barged to this area in the early 1900s and possibly used in a nearby quarry (McDonald and Lahore 1994).

Figure 34—A stark reminder of the demise of the Leach lumber operation was the deteriorating Owl Gulch mill and flume. Compare the structures in this photo to those in figure 9.

Although the cab was gone, the similarity of engine type and design, the timing of departure from Owl Gulch and arrival near San Rafael, and the lack of any other 0-6-0 tender locomotive for use in California by Baldwin in the 1880s, suggest that this was the final resting place for the locomotive of the Challenge Mill railroad.

Not all was completely lost when the flume and the railroad were no longer used, however, because boards and rails from them still had value. A local correspondent remembered seeing "a bar made out of a single 30-inch-wide gorgeous sugar pine board from Leach's flume." Another remembered his father getting boards from the flume to build part of a fence near his house. Later he built his barn with some flume boards. Still another stated "We got lumber out of the flume and built a chicken house. Everybody in the whole country up here got lumber out of the flume to build buildings on their places." In the 1920s, a few hardrock mines above Challenge were still working and when rails were needed in their tunnels, they were salvaged from the old railroad.

By then, most of the mines had closed and the timber harvested. Farmers also departed, finding much to their sorrow that late spring frosts and hot dry summers made farming a fruitless enterprise. Buildings in Challenge declined as they weathered, were moved elsewhere, burned, or torn down. However, the Challenge store persisted along with a few smaller and temporary businesses, selling goods and services to an occasional hunter, fisherman, hopeful miner, or a few loggers traveling to higher elevations. Not until the Great Depression of the 1930s did

Challenge again awaken as desperate men eked out an existence "sniping" for gold in Dry Creek, Oregon Creek, and other streams. Today, all businesses are closed, and the few remaining old homes, unless restored, are falling into disrepair. All that remains of Challenge is a school that serves it and five neighboring towns, a Post Office, a U.S. Forest Service work station, and two churches.

Acknowledgments

The authors interviewed many gracious oldtimers who laboriously searched their memories for the events in their lives that gave us this history. It is mostly their stories and photos that we present. In alphabetical order they are:

Adams, Charles (Bud)	Kelley, Arta
Ahart, Pete	Kelly, Earnest
Bird, John	Kumle, Mabel
Chittenden, Warren	Moran, Alex
Costa, Tony and Effie	Nelson, Ralph
Cummings, Ruth	Pauly, Arvid
Donald, Ray	Taylor, Ben and Ruth
Gordon, Ray Sr.	Travis, Margie
Heenan, Edna (Kelly)	Veercamp, Worthy
Keith, E.F.	Wedgeworth, Bill

Special thanks and recognition are given to Rosemarie Mossinger of the Yuba-Feather Historical Museum who gave us much needed advice, supplied several valuable photos, and kindly reviewed this manuscript.

In spite of constant checking and laborious cross correlating, some discrepancies exist and some conflicts remain unsolved. We have strived to keep our material in the 1875 to 1910 period and some confusion has arisen because changes were made during this timeframe. Hence a home was given a family name in one interview and a different one in another. Both probably are correct. It is our hope that readers will be tolerant and only smile if a discrepancy is found.

Literature Cited

Bancroft, H.H. 1890. The Works XXIV. History of California. Volume 7, 1860–1890. 826 p.

Bean, W. 1970. The Vee Flume. Typewritten copy on file with the Pacific Southwest Forest and Range Experiment Station, 3644 Avtech Parkway, Redding, CA 96002. 5 p.

Chamberlain, W.H.; Wells, H.L. 1879. History of Yuba County. Oakland, CA: Thompson and West: 92–96.

Cronise, T.F. 1868. The natural wealth of California. San Francisco, CA: H.H. Bancroft & Company. 642 p.

General Services Administration, National Archives and Records Service. 1975. (May 1). Letter to Ms. Lurene Williams, Challenge, CA. On file with: Pacific Southwest Forest and Range Experiment Station, 3644 Avtech Parkway, Redding, CA 96002.

Kroeber, A.L. 1976. Handbook of the Indians of California. New York: Dover Publications, Inc. 429–431.

Leach, F.P. 1925. Lawrence Leach of Salem, Massachusetts, and some of his descendants. Volume II. St. Albans, VT: The Messenger Press. 1002 p.

Mansfield, G.C. 1918. History of Butte County, California. Los Angeles, CA: Historic Record Company: 283–284.

McDonald, P.M.; Lahore, L.F. 1984. Lumbering in the northern Sierra Nevada: Andrew Martin Leach of Challenge Mills. The Pacific Historian. 28(2): 19–31.

McDonald, P.M.; Lahore, L.F. 1994. The Challenge Mill railroad. The Californians. 11(3): 40–43.

Mossinger, R. 2006. Images of America: Yuba Feather Hills. San Francisco, CA: Arcadia Publishing. 128 p.

Pacific Coast Wood and Iron. 1887. 8(5): 71.

Pacific Coast Wood and Iron. 1893. 20(2): 70.

Thompson and West Document. 1879. (April 14). (microfilm #134). Letter to H.S. Wells from A.P. Willey. Yuba County Library, 303 2nd Street, Marysville, CA 95901.

Williams, C.E. 1887. Yuba and Sutter Counties, California. San Francisco, CA: Bacon and Company. 33–35.